ABOUT THIS STUDY:

You have a game face... likely several of them. It's the part of you that you let others see. It changes some depending on who is around and what the situation is. Everybody plays the game and everybody knows it.

So do you have a game face for God? Are there parts of your heart, soul and mind that are "off-limits" for Him? In one sense it's ridiculous. In another sense, you know that's how you play the spiritual game to one extent or another. After all, if God had to wade through your junk it might stain His holiness or something. Your rational mind says He takes a long walk when your path gets messy because somehow He is too pure to deal with your muddy boots. Just like if the people around you saw the messy parts inside you they wouldn't trust you to lead or minister to them.

Psalm 139 takes that concept of God and turns it on its head. He is intensely personal. He sees it all. He's there when it happens. He knows you inside out. And He is still walking the path with you regardless. Maybe the real question is whether you are ready to drop the game face with Him and find freedom in being transparent.

TRANSPARENT

PSALM 139

ontrack devotions
EXPEDITION

www.OnTrackDevotions.com

OnTrack Expedition: Transparent: Psalm 139

Printed in the United States of America

Copyright © 2015 Pilgrimage Educational Resources

Any internet addresses, email addresses, phone numbers and physical addresses in this book are accurate at the time of publication. They are
provided as a resource. Pilgrimage Educational Resources does not endorse them or vouch for their content or permanence.

Author: Dwight E. Peterson
Executive Developer: Benjamin J. Wilhite
Graphic design by Lance Young (higherrockcreative.com)

ISBN-13 978-0692478752
ISBN 0692478752

10 9 8 7 6 5 4 3 2 1

PSALM 139 (ESV)

To the choirmaster. A Psalm of David.

1 O LORD, you have searched me and known me! 2 You know when I sit down and when I rise up; you discern my thoughts from afar. 3 You search out my path and my lying down and are acquainted with all my ways. 4 Even before a word is on my tongue, behold, O LORD, you know it altogether. 5 You hem me in, behind and before, and lay your hand upon me. 6 Such knowledge is too wonderful for me; it is high; I cannot attain it.

7 Where shall I go from your Spirit? Or where shall I flee from your presence? 8 If I ascend to heaven, you are there! If I make my bed in Sheol, you are there! 9 If I take the wings of the morning and dwell in the uttermost parts of the sea, 10 even there your hand shall lead me, and your right hand shall hold me. 11 If I say, "Surely the darkness shall cover me, and the light about me be night," 12 even the darkness is not dark to you; the night is bright as the day, for darkness is as light with you.

13 For you formed my inward parts; you knitted me together in my mother's womb. 14 I praise you, for I am fearfully and wonderfully made. Wonderful are your works; my soul knows it very well. 15 My frame was not hidden from you, when I was being made in secret, intricately woven in the depths of the earth. 16 Your eyes saw my unformed substance;in your book were written, every one of them, the days that were formed for me, when as yet there was none of them.

17 How precious to me are your thoughts, O God! How vast is the sum of them! 18 If I would count them, they are more than the sand. I awake, and I am still with you.

19 Oh that you would slay the wicked, O God! O men of blood, depart from me! 20 They speak against you with malicious intent; your enemies take your name in vain! 21 Do I not hate those who hate you, O LORD? And do I not loathe those who rise up against you? 22 I hate them with complete hatred; I count them my enemies.

23 Search me, O God, and know my heart! Try me and know my thoughts! 24 And see if there be any grievous way in me, and lead me in the way everlasting!

PASSAGE
INTRO NOTES

Record key ideas from the passage introduction or from your first read through the entire passage. Write down any "big questions" on the tag below so you can revisit them during the week.

oʇd
EXPEDITION

BIG questions this week...

1: SET GOALS

This exercise is designed to help prepare your heart and mind for the week of your upcoming event. Take some time to get alone and answer them. Good goals should be specific and measurable.

(1) Complete the following sentences to help you formulate some goals for the week:

This week, I hope I...

This week, I hope we as a group...

(2) Complete the following sentences to help you begin to formulate a strategy for seeing the above goals fulfilled:

In light of my answers above, I must...

In light of my answers above, we must...

(3) Complete the following sentences to help you formulate a plan to avoid what will derail your goals:

In light of my answers, I must not...

In light of my answers, we must not...

2: PLAN & COMMIT

Take your responses from the previous questions and write out a "personal commitment" for the week. That is, what are you going to personally commit to be doing this week and commit to not be doing. You will sign it and seek out at least one other person on the trip who will read it, pray for its fulfillment, and keep you accountable to it. If possible, seek out a second witness that will not be part of the event group that will pray for you during the event and will check in with you afterward to see how it went.

I, _____, personally commit to

I further commit to not

Name: _____

Signature: _____

Witness#1: _____

Witness#2: _____

Date: ___/___/___

1ST DAY
KNOWN

1: JOURNAL

Experiences
What experiences have you faced in the last 24 hours?

Questions
What questions do you find yourself asking?

Conclusions
What kind of conclusions are you coming to about yourself and others?

oad
EXPEDITION

2: READ PSALM 139
Read through the entire chapter and record any thoughts or questions which are generated from what you read. In addition, record how the content relates to what you are dealing with on this week.

3: EVALUATE
Answer the questions below based on Psalm 136:1-6.

What do we mean when we say God is Omniscient?

In what ways does this attribute impact your life today? In your daily life back home?

How should this attribute impact your desire for God to search you?

In what ways have your responses demonstrated that you are or are not living with an awareness of God's omniscience?

In what ways can you be more aware for the remainder of the week?

4: INTEGRATE
Spend some time on each of the following activities to get the most out of today's study.

Memorize Psalm 139:23-24

Pray
Spend some time praying for yourself and for others in your group.

Commit
In light of what you see in yourself so far, what personal commitment will you make for today? Write it down...

Today, I'm praying for...

I commit to...

1: JOURNAL

Experiences
What experiences have you faced in the last 24 hours?

Questions
What questions do you find yourself asking?

Conclusions
What kind of conclusions are you coming to about yourself and others?

O⳨d
EXPEDITION

2: READ PSALM 139
Read through the entire chapter and record any thoughts or questions which are generated from what you read. In addition, record how the content relates to what you are dealing with on this week.

3: EVALUATE

Answer the questions below based on Psalm 139:7-12.

What do we mean when we say God is Omnipresent?

In what ways does this attribute impact your life today? In your daily life back home?

How should this attribute impact your desire for God to search you?

In what ways have your responses demonstrated that you are or are not living with an awareness of God's omnipresence?

In what ways can you be more aware for the remainder of the week?

4: INTEGRATE

Spend some time on each of the following activities to get the most out of today's study.

Memorize Psalm 139:23-24

Pray
Spend some time praying for yourself and for others in your group.

Commit
In light of what you see in yourself so far, what personal commitment will you make for today? Write it down...

Today, I'm praying for...

I commit to...

1: JOURNAL

Experiences
What experiences have you faced in the last 24 hours?

Questions
What questions do you find yourself asking?

Conclusions
What kind of conclusions are you coming to about yourself and others?

O+d
EXPEDITION

2: READ PSALM 139
Read through the entire chapter and record any thoughts or questions which are generated from what you read. In addition, record how the content relates to what you are dealing with on this week.

3: EVALUATE

Answer the questions below based on Psalm 139:13-22.

What do we mean when we say God is the creator of all things?

What do we mean when we say God is holy?

In what ways do these attributes impact your life today? In your daily life back home?

How should these attributes impact your desire for God to search you?

In what ways have your responses demonstrated that you are or are not living with an awareness of God as our holy creator?

In what ways can you be more aware for the remainder of the week?

4: INTEGRATE

Spend some time on each of the following activities to get the most out of today's study.

Memorize Psalm 139:23-24

Pray
Spend some time praying for yourself and for others in your group.

Commit
In light of what you see in yourself so far, what personal commitment will you make for today? Write it down...

Today, I'm praying for...

I commit to...

4TH DAY
SHAME

1: JOURNAL

Experiences
What experiences have you faced in the last 24 hours?

Questions
What questions do you find yourself asking?

Conclusions
What kind of conclusions are you coming to about yourself and others?

O4D
EXPEDITION

2: READ LUKE 5:1-11
Read through the entire section and record any thoughts or questions which are generated from what you read. In addition, record how the content relates to what you are dealing with on this week.

3: EVALUATE
Answer the questions below based on Luke 5:1-11.

What attributes did Christ demonstrate to Peter in this section of Scripture?

How does Peter's response to those attributes differ from David's in Psalm 139?

In what ways do you see yourself responding like Peter or David to God's attributes?

What can you do to allow God's attributes to lead you to David's response, not Peters?

4: INTEGRATE
Spend some time on each of the following activities to get the most out of today's study.

Memorize Psalm 139:23-24

Pray
Spend some time praying for yourself and for others in your group.

Commit
In light of what you see in yourself so far, what personal commitment will you make for today? Write it down...

Today, I'm praying for...

I commit to...

1: JOURNAL

Experiences
What experiences have you faced in the last 24 hours?

Questions
What questions do you find yourself asking?

Conclusions
What kind of conclusions are you coming to about yourself and others?

OFD
EXPEDITION

2: READ PSALM 139
Read through the entire chapter and record any thoughts or questions which are generated from what you read. In addition, record how the content relates to what you are dealing with on this week.

3: EVALUATE
Answer the questions below based on Psalm 139:23-24.

Why, if God has already "searched" and "known" the psalmist (v. 1) do you think he ends the passage asking God to do it again?

Even though the writer already acknowledged God's presence and protection (v. 5), why do you think he continues to have "thougts" that required "searching?"

How do you think his "thoughts" are related to God "trying" him? How does that concept connect to your experiences so far this week?

Are you willing to ask God to search, try and lead you... to be transparent to Him? What does that look like as you get ready to wrap up this week?

4: INTEGRATE
Spend some time on each of the following activities to get the most out of today's study.

Memorize Psalm 139:23-24

Pray
Spend some time praying for yourself and for others in your group.

Commit
In light of what you see in yourself so far, what personal commitment will you make for today? Write it down...

Today, I'm praying for...

I commit to...

1: EVALUATE

This exercise is designed to help discover and record the key takeaways from the week. Take some time to work through the process so you will get the most out of it.

(1) Take some time to read back through the pre trip contract you signed at the beginning of the week.

Write down some of the occasions where you fulfilled your commitment this week.

Write down some of the occasions where you struggled with your commitment this week.

List some of the experiences God used this week to challenge you in light of your commitment.

(2) Read back through your daily journal entries and Bible study notes and answer the questions below.

Which of the four attributes of God challenged you the most this week?

...Why?

In light of what you have learned from Psalm 139, what changes are you determined to make?

What specific plans can you implement in order to see those changes become a reality?

How can you involve others?

2: APPLY

This exercise is designed to help connect your key takeaways to "real life" at home. Take some time to work through each of the steps below.

(1) Take a minute and think about what things will be like when you get home. Write down your thoughts.

What are you most looking forward to?

What are you least looking forward to?

(2) Where do you think it'll be most difficult to live out what you've learned?

(3) Where do you think it will be easiest to live out what you've learned?

3: COMMIT

Take your responses from the previous questions and write out a "personal commitment" for your transition to "real life." That is, what are you going to personally commit to be doing and commit to not be doing at home. You will sign it and seek out at least one other person from the trip who will read it, pray for its fulfillment, and keep you accountable to it. Also seek out a key person at home to share your commitment(s) with that will encourage you, pray for you and hold you accountable.

I, _____, personally commit to

I further commit to not

Name: _____

Signature: _____

Witness#1: _____

Witness#2: _____

Date: ___/___/___

MEET THE AUTHOR

Since 1985, Dwight Peterson has been an integral part of the mission and ministry of Pilgrimage Educational Resources. After serving for three years as Youth Pastor at Brookdale Baptist Church (Bloomfield, NJ), Dwight accepted the Youth Pastor role at First Baptist Church (Elkhart, IN), where he served for 14 years. His area of responsibility included junior high, senior high and college ministry along with oversight of the Bible curriculum and discipleship functions at the Christian school operated by the church. In Elkhart, Dwight developed training courses for his youth ministry teams while also making them available in workshop and written formats as curriculum to other youth ministries. Out of this, he created and has continuously developed OnTrack Devotions.

Currently, Mr. Peterson serves on the faculty of Summit University (Clarks Summit, PA) as well as carrying various responsibilities at PER. Dwight's goal at BBC, with Pilgrimage, or in everyday life is to disciple students. Whether that be in his Youth Ministry classes, leading a wilderness trip, coaching, or hanging out with the guys in the dorm, where he serves as Resident Director, growth is the end goal. For the past several years, Dwight has also been directing the TLC Youth Workers Conference.

Dwight Peterson

Role: Wilderness Institute Director

Where: Pilgrimage Educational Resources

Family: Married w/4 children and 6 grandchildren

Online: OnTrackDevotions.com

EDITION

"One of the most effective tools for changing lives I have ever seen... the perfect environment for God to work resulting in permanent life change."

WILDERNESS INSTITUTE FOR LEADERSHIP DEVELOPMENT

W.I.L.D.

SIMPLYPILGRIM.COM

OCTOBER
★ ★ ★ ★

FEBRUARY
★ ★ ★ ★

THE ONTRACK DEVOTIONS MILITARY EDITION IS A 12-MONTH STUDY THROUGH THE NEW TESTAMENT AND PROVERBS WRITTEN FOR TODAY'S MILITARY PERSONNEL. THE INCLUDED USER GUIDE WALKS THE READER THROUGH THE BASIC STEPS OF INDUCTIVE BIBLE STUDY (OBSERVATION, INTERPRETATION, APPLICATION, IMPLEMENTATION), ALLOWING THEM TO START AT THEIR CURRENT SKILL LEVEL AND DIVE INTO THE MEAT OF THE WORD OF GOD.

WHETHER YOU ARE A CHAPLAIN LOOKING FOR RESOURCES FOR YOUR UNIT, A CHURCH WITH ACTIVE DUTY MEMBERS OR A SOLDIER, SAILOR, AIRMAN OR MARINE THAT NEEDS A FIELD-READY DEVOTIONAL GUIDE, MOTD FITS THE BILL. THE YEAR IS BROKEN DOWN INTO 12 ONE-MONTH SECTIONS WITH A USER GUIDE THAT INTRODUCES THE "WHY" AND "HOW" OF INDUCTIVE BIBLE STUDY.

FOLLOW AND LIKE MILITARY DEVOS FOR DAILY DEVO THOUGHTS:

🐦 @MILITARYDEVOS

📘 FACEBOOK.COM/MILITARYDEVOS

MILITARYDEVOTIONAL.COM

PILGRIMAGE EDUCATIONAL RESOURCES
1362 FORDS POND RD
CLARKS SUMMIT, PA 18411